110104831

10420

Jenks East Elementary School D

PEDAL POWER

THE HISTORY OF BICYCLES

Peter Lafferty and David Jefferis

Franklin Watts
New York London Toronto Sydney

Illustrated by
Robert Burns
Chris Forsey
Ron Jobson
Michael Roffe

Photographs supplied by
Allsport
Norman Barrett
Mary Evans Picture Library
David Jefferis

Technical consultant
Patrick Devereaux

© 1990 Franklin Watts

Franklin Watts Inc.
387 Park Avenue South
New York, NY 10016

Printed in Belgium

All rights reserved

Library of Congress Cataloging-in-Publication data

Lafferty, Peter.
Pedal Power : the history of bicycles / Peter Lafferty and David Jefferis.
p. cm – – (Wheels)
Summary: Traces the use of bicycles from their origins to the present day, with competitive racing and all-terrain bikes.
ISBN 0–531–14084–9
1. Bicycles – History – Juvenile literature. [1. Bicycles and bicycling.] I. Jefferis. David. II. Title. III. Series.
TL400.L33 1990
629.227'2'09 –dc20

89–39669
CIP AC

PEDAL POWER

Contents

Introduction

The story of the bicycle goes back some 200 years. In 1791, the French Count de Sivrac delighted onlookers in a Paris park as he showed off his two-wheeled invention, a machine he called the "celerifere." It was basically an enlarged version of a children's toy which had been in use for many years.

Sivrac's celerifere had a wooden frame, carved to look like a horse, mounted to a wheel at either end. To ride it, you sat astride the frame and pushed hard against the ground with your legs.

The celerifere had no steering, but despite this caught on with the fashionable young men of Paris. Soon they were holding races up and down the Champs Elysees, one of the biggest Parisian boulevards. Minor injuries were common as riders attempted a final burst of speed. Turns caused problems, as the only way to change direction was to heave up the "neck" of the celerifere and swing the machine around while the front wheel was spinning in the air.

Celeriferes proved a passing craze however, as the combination of no springs, no steering and rough roads made riding them very uncomfortable. Even so, the wooden celerifere was the ancestor of the modern bicycle.

Today's bikes are among the most efficient machines ever made. A cyclist can travel about 2,500 km (1,600 miles) on the food energy equivalent to that of 4.5 liters (1 gallon) of gasoline. Even an economical small car can only cover 80 km (50 miles) or so on this amount. In cities which are heavily congested with traffic, bicycle journeys are often quicker than the same ones driven in cars. And bicycles produce no polluting engine exhaust fumes.

▷ The Count de Sivrac's celerifere. The wheels were made of wood, like the coach wheels of the day. The wheels were fitted with iron hoops for tires, held in place with nails. To turn a celerifere you had to pull a "wheelie" – lift the front wheel off the ground, while swinging the machine around on its back wheel.

High tech bikes of today

The modern bicycle is the result of a long period of refining the basic design. By carefully selecting the frame, gears and other components, a bike can be as precisely tailored to its rider as a handmade suit of clothes. Bicycles fall into several major groups – racing machines, tourers, small wheel shoppers and tough all-terrain bikes, suitable for off-road work. The bike shown here is a classic touring machine, complete with typical components, including drop handlebars and lightweight frame.

Touring bicycle

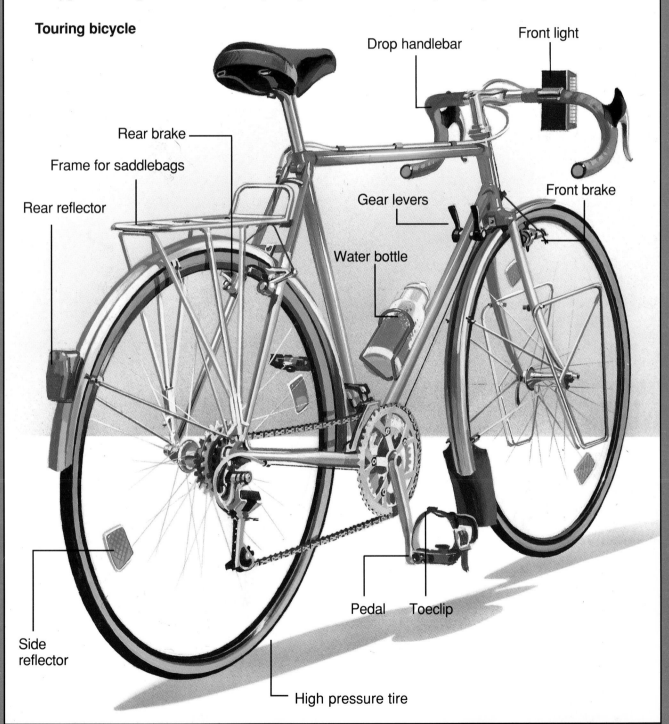

Drop handlebar

Front light

Rear brake

Frame for saddlebags

Rear reflector

Gear levers

Front brake

Water bottle

Side reflector

Pedal   Toeclip

High pressure tire

The baron's running machine

In 1817, a German baron, Karl von Drais, made a two-wheeler which he called a "draisienne." It looked very similar to a celerifere, but the baron made an important improvement – he added a steering arrangement for the front wheel. He also fitted a cushioned saddle and a rest for his arms and chest.

Von Drais worked as chief forest ranger for the Grand Duke of Baden and used his draisienne for patrolling the woods. Once he rode from Karlsruhe to the nearby town of Schweizingen in an hour. This mostly downhill journey took three hours or more to walk, and made an ideal course for the draisienne.

In 1818, von Drais took his machine to Paris. The draisienne caught on immediately

▽ Baron von Drais, patrolling his machine through the woods. Using his steering tiller, the baron could avoid running into the bumps and gulleys of the forest paths.

and with good reason, for it was the fastest vehicle on the road. Races against horse-drawn carriages proved no contest – the draisienne could outpace them all.

Draisiennes caught on in Britain and America too, where they were known as "dandy horses" after the rich young men, or dandies, who rode them. Other names included the "pedestrian hobby horse" and the "swiftwalker." In France the machines were called velocipedes, meaning "fast feet," and this term became the word mostly used to describe these leg-propelled bikes.

The general public was irritated by the antics of the riders who often took little notice of other people in their way. They usually rode on footpaths, which were smoother than the roads of the time. Velocipede riders, who looked rather undignified as they wobbled along, were made the object of jokes and cartoons. The ridicule was enough to persuade most riders to drop their new sport, and by the early 1820s, the hobby horse craze was over.

△ Special schools were set up to teach people how to ride the new machines. This picture shows Johnson's Pedestrian Hobby Horse School in London. Here, learning riders practiced around a small dirt track, while an instructor shouted out orders to them.

△ Velocipede riding was an almost entirely male affair. Women wore long dresses which made it impossible to ride a velocipede. One solution was this ladies' hobby horse of 1819. Using a treadle and handgrip system for power, a lady rider could move the machine along slowly.

From feet to pedals

Ideas for adding power to the velocipede were many and varied. Among the early efforts was that of Lewis Gompertz of Surrey, England. His 1821 machine had a curved handlebar set in front of a chest rail. When the bar was pulled, the teeth mounted at its bottom end turned the front wheel.

A few years later, in 1840, Scotsman Kirkpatrick Macmillan produced a hobby horse with pedals. Looking like stirrups, the pedals were attached to long rods which turned the back wheel. The velocipede couldn't change direction very well, and this fault may have helped cause the first known serious bicycle accident. In 1842, Macmillan went on a 64 km (40 mile) trip to Glasgow. On the outskirts of the town, he plowed into a crowd of people,

knocking over a small child. Later, in court, he was found guilty and fined twenty-five cents. The judge was so interested in the velocipede however, that he paid the fine in return for a demonstration!

It was not until the 1860s that a really popular pedal-powered machine was built. Pierre and Ernest Michaux were a father and son team, making baby carriages, wheelchairs and three-wheelers in Paris. They improved the basic draisienne design by fitting an iron frame, a saddle and pedals on the front wheel. Though the saddle was comfortable, the wheels were metal and there were no springs, so the Michaux soon became known as the "boneshaker." Even so, the French machine had so many good points that bicycling as a sport and means of local transportation took off in a big way.

△ Kirkpatrick MacMillan's hobby horse. The foot treadles were linked to the back wheel by a pair of metal rods.

▷ This 1868 boneshaker includes several advanced features. The saddle is mounted on a metal spring for comfort. Solid rubber tires give a better ride than metal hoops. The bike also has a brake. Pulling on a handlebar cord forced a metal shoe against the rear tire, to slow the bike. The pedals were joined directly to the front axle, with no gears.

Metal brake shoe

Riding the high wheel

Michaux bicycles were popular but fairly slow. This was because they had no gears. The pedals were attached to the front wheel and one turn of the pedals took the machine only a short distance.

James Starley of Coventry, England, improved the top speed of his 1870 Ariel bicycle by increasing the size of the front wheel. A turn of the pedals took a rider much further than when on a Michaux. The Ariel was also lightweight and had wire spoked wheels similar to those of today. With its low weight and high speed, the Ariel started a performance race between bicycle manufacturers and soon all the top machines shared the large front "high wheel" design. James Moore, a famous racer, bought a high wheel and achieved over 22 km/h (14 mph).

High wheel bikes became so common they were known as "ordinaries." They were not popular with everyone though. In 1876, a London buggy driver lashed out at an overtaking cyclist with his whip. The conductor joined in the attack by throwing a

△ The American Star of 1881 was an attempt to produce a safer bike than the standard ordinary. Its small front wheel stopped it from pitching forward down slopes. The Star's safety was shown during a bumpy demonstration ride down the steps of the Capitol building in Washington, D.C.

large iron ball on the end of a rope into the spokes of the bicycle. The cyclist overturned and was dragged along behind the buggy until the rope snapped. In court, the fine was so small that bicycle riders were convinced

that the police were against them too!

Riding an ordinary was exhilarating, even if you came across no attackers. Sitting over a front wheel anything up to 152 cm (5 ft) in diameter gave a splendid view over hedges and walls. Going down hills took courage though, since any serious braking could send you hurtling over the handlebars. Despite the dangers, many cycling clubs were formed. Several were run on military lines, with strict riding rules.

△ This group of ordinary riders was featured in the pages of the 1874 *Graphic* newspaper.

▽ Riding an ordinary was no easy matter. A wall was useful to lean on if you had no helper. Otherwise you had two methods of getting aboard. You could run beside the bike, put a foot on the metal step above the small wheel, swing up your other leg and climb into the saddle. A more difficult way of mounting was to start with a foot on the step and hop along until you had enough speed to get into the saddle. Getting off was easier, but with a big drop to the ground!

Safety bicycles

If you weren't brave or sporting enough to ride an ordinary, then you had to turn to a tricycle or quadricycle. There were plenty to choose from – James Starley even presented one to Queen Victoria, who reportedly enjoyed riding it very much. But the hunt was on for a better two-wheel machine than the ordinary.

In 1884, James Starley's nephew, John, produced the Rover "safety" bicycle. The pedals were no longer directly connected to the wheel and had a geared chain drive for easy starts and good hill climbing. Rider George Smith proved the performance of the second Rover safety with a record time of just over seven hours to cover a 160 km (100 mile) course. The invention of the safety spelled doom for the ordinary. Outclassed and outperformed, ordinaries were nicknamed "penny-farthings," a scornful name for their last years. With the development of the safety, women took up cycling in a big way. A safety could be ridden even when a lady was wearing one of the long dresses in fashion at the time.

The next great cycling invention was the air-filled pneumatic tire. Its inventor was a Scotsman, John Boyd Dunlop. Cycle racers found Dunlop's invention helped them win races; the new tires enabled them to ride faster and more comfortably than when they used solid rubber tires. In a few years, pneumatic tires had replaced solids.

▽ Alternatives to the rather dangerous ordinary included cycles with three or four wheels. Versions were made which could take one, two or more people in stately comfort. They were also good load carriers.

▷ The first Rover safety bicycle was an odd-looking contraption, with a big front wheel and set-back handlebars. A second design was much more modern, though it had an oddly curved frame.

The pneumatic tire

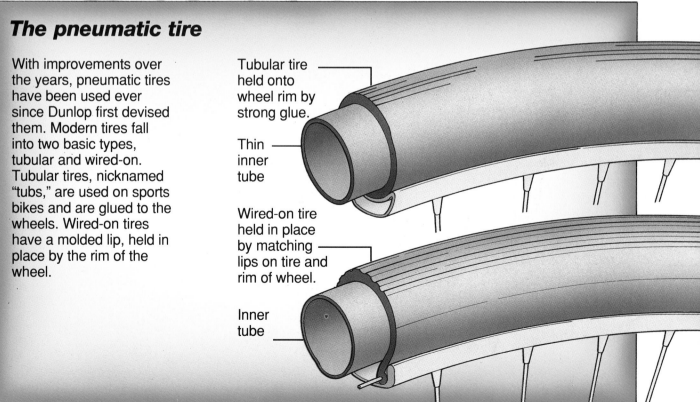

With improvements over the years, pneumatic tires have been used ever since Dunlop first devised them. Modern tires fall into two basic types, tubular and wired-on. Tubular tires, nicknamed "tubs," are used on sports bikes and are glued to the wheels. Wired-on tires have a molded lip, held in place by the rim of the wheel.

Tubular tire held onto wheel rim by strong glue.

Thin inner tube

Wired-on tire held in place by matching lips on tire and rim of wheel.

Inner tube

Into the modern age

In the early 1900s, more improvements were made to the bicycle. The freewheel mechanism, which allowed pedals to stay still while the bike coasted along was introduced. Brakes, tires and frame designs were all improved. Most important of all, gears were fitted which took some of the hard work out of climbing hills, and allowed high top speeds.

The Sturmey-Archer hub gear was first fitted to a bicycle by the Raleigh Cycle Company in 1902. The simple three-speed design remains much the same today. Derailleur gears, which allow a huge range of speeds, were also introduced. They work as the French name indicates, by "derailing" the chain from one set of gear cogs to another. Low gears are used for starts and hills, high gears for cycling on flat surfaces or downhill. Advantages of derailleur gears include low weight and easy adjustment. Caliper brakes were a big improvement upon earlier types. They use a pair of hard rubber blocks to grip each side of the wheel, giving smooth and well-controlled braking.

These technical improvements ensured the continued success of the bicycle. Bikes were used by doctors, policemen, mailmen and for people to cycle to work. In the 1920s, there was still a strong interest in bicycling for sport and leisure, though automobiles were becoming cheaper and more popular. In countries such as the United States, many people could afford their own cars for the first time and popular interest in bicycling went into a long decline. In other countries, people still depended on bicycles as a basic means of transportation.

▷ Pedal deliveries were popular in the 1920s and 1930s. Tricycles, with load compartments between the front wheels, made ideal trade vehicles. They were sturdy, with thick, almost puncture-proof tires. They were used for mail deliveries, by ice cream vendors, chimney sweeps and many others. The boys that pedaled the heavy machines either loved or hated their mounts. If they were ambitious cyclists, no weather was too cold or wet. For others, the work was a hard, daily grind.

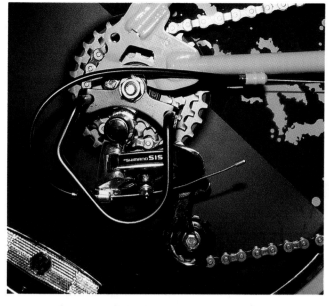

△ Hub gears, generally with three speeds, are reliable and long lasting. The sealed mechanism only needs occasional oiling and adjusting.

The drawback is a loss of efficiency, with only about 50 percent of a cyclist's pedaling power being converted to movement of the back wheel.

△ Derailleur gears are by far the most popular for use on enthusiast bikes. Tourers typically have ten speeds, mountain bikes 15 to 21. When they are

properly adjusted, derailleurs are very efficient, transmitting over 90 percent of a cyclist's effort on the pedals to movement of the rear wheel.

Bicycles at war

In 1900, bicycles were used as scouting vehicles during the Boer War in South Africa. On the wide plains of the African veldt, they were ideal, but were less useful in hilly areas.

Later, in World War I, at least one army formed a bicycle corps. Bikes had handlebar clips to hold rifles. In World War II, special folding bikes were developed for airborne troops. The bicycle soldier shown here was one of the many thousands of men taken into battle

by troop-carrying gliders. In the Vietnam War of the 1960s and 1970s, communist troops used bicycles by the thousand, to carry weapons and material along jungle trails, from North Vietnam to southern battle areas. Because the cycle tracks were narrow and well hidden, it was an almost impossible job to stop the deliveries. Even large weapons ended up on bicycles. They were broken down into their component parts and reassembled on delivery.

Small wheel bikes

Between the 1930s and 1950s, bicycle design changed very little, with only minor improvements in basic equipment and layout. Then, in 1962, English engineer Alex Moulton came up with the first completely new bicycle design since Starley's 1884 safety bike.

The Moulton bike had tiny wheels, just 41 cm (16 in) across, instead of the more usual 66 cm (26 in). The small wheel design had several advantages, including a light frame and good maneuverability. Small wheels were not so good at absorbing bumps as bigger wheels though, but Moulton overcame this problem by fitting rubber shock absorbers in the front and rear.

Since Moulton's first machine, small wheeled bikes have become popular, mainly as general purpose runabouts. Most have a quick-change lever system to raise or lower the seat and handlebars. This makes a single bike suitable for all the family, at least for shopping trips and occasional leisure runs.

Other small wheel bikes have since included "choppers," which were popular in the 1970s. These were styled after the Harley-Davidson customized motorcycles of the period. In the 1970s and 1980s, BMX took off in a big way. Bicycle motocross let cycle racing take place off the road, on dirt racetracks. Freestyling enabled skilled BMX riders to show off the art of making their bikes do a range of amazing tricks.

With BMX bikes came an exciting range of high-style accessories, from molded handlebar grips to colorful license plates. Modern design had come cycling.

Today's mountain bikes use a mid-size wheel, bigger than a BMX but smaller than a tourer, for the roughest off-road action.

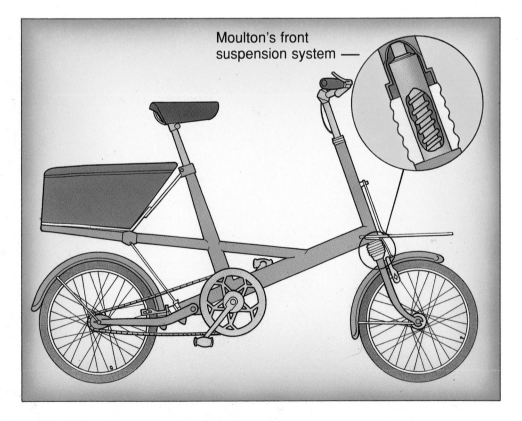

Moulton's front suspension system —

◁ The Moulton's unique suspension system gives a good ride over rough surfaces. Cheaper bikes mostly have "balloon" tires, using their bigger size to absorb the bumps. This makes such machines more difficult to ride, as wide tires need more push than narrow, high pressure types.

From shopper to dirt rider

These bikes cover a wide range of small wheel designs. The shopping bike is useful for a family to use on short local trips. The high tech Strida can be packed into a car and used for country sightseeing. The BMX is a racer, built for toughness and speed.

Low adjustment

High adjustment

△ Shopping bikes typically have 51 cm (20 in) wheels, with carrying case in the front and rear to carry packages. Seat and handlebar height can be changed in a few seconds.

▷ The 1986 Strida weighs just 10 kg (22 lb). Made of aluminum alloy and plastics, the Strida needs no oiling or greasing. It can be folded up in seven seconds. It only has a single speed however, which limits its use to fairly flat country.

◁ BMX bikes were designed as dirt racers, with knobby tires to give a good grip on dirt and gravel. Much new technology went into the bikes, including frames made of "Cro-mo," a strong chrome molybdenum material similar to aircraft tubing.

Tour de France

Racing has been popular ever since the early days of cycling. The first race took place in Paris in 1868. Today France remains the home of cycle racing, with the world's best known event, the Tour de France, taking place every year. The route, about 4,000 km (2,400 miles) long, changes each time but always ends in Paris. The race takes some three weeks, with riders covering stages of 200 km (120 miles) or so each day.

The 1904 Tour was possibly the most chaotic race of all time. Some riders were given drugged water by their rivals and one man crashed when he fell asleep in the saddle after sleeping pills had been dissolved in his drink. Another rider crashed because the frame of his bike had been filed through. There was even a rider who had his shirt filled with itching powder! Nails were thrown on the roads, causing many punctures and crashes. During one night run,

the race leaders were attacked by a gang of one hundred men armed with sticks and rocks. Only the arrival of the police, firing pistols into the air, saved the frightened racers. "The Tour is finished," moaned race organizer Henri Desgranges after the race. He was wrong of course, as the Tour de France is still going strong, and is more popular than ever.

Other cycle sports include track racing, which takes place on specially-built sloping oval circuits. Cyclo-cross is racing across rough country. Riders have to judge whether it's quicker to pedal or carry their bikes over steep or muddy sections.

Amateur riders can enjoy cycle sports too. There are events of all kinds, whether you wish to road race or ride your mountain bike. Among the toughest events are triathlons, which combine cycling with running and swimming.

◁ Cyclo-cross demands speed, strength and a tough bike. A typical course includes slippery muddy paths, steep climbs and descents, and a stream crossing. A winning cyclo-crosser has to be a strong runner as well as a fast cyclist, and know when it's best to pick up the bike and run with it.

△ The Tour de France covers all types of country, from plains to mountains. Along the way, there are various prizes for special sections. "King of the mountain" is the title earned by the first rider up the steepest peak.

◁ Pursuit bikes are computer-designed for maximum performance. The frame is sized to match the rider and shaped to reduce wind resistance. Wheels are often spokeless disks, made of strong but light carbon based material.

19

Mountain bikes

The development of mountain bikes, or ATB all-terrain bicycles, began in the hills just north of San Francisco, California, in the mid-1970s. A band of enthusiastic cyclists began racing down the steep trails. There were no ready-to-buy machines able to handle the rough terrain, so if you wanted to race, then you had to build your own bike, matching old-fashioned wide tires and frame to modern derailleur gears. Bikes like this were known as "clunkers," because compared to lightweight road and track racers, they looked heavy and unwieldy.

The most famous clunker race was the super-steep Repack, named because bikes which used hub brakes had to be repacked with fresh oil at the end. The Repack run was about 3 km (2 miles) long, during which riders descended 394 m (1,300 ft). The route included ruts and rocks, blind corners, soft ground, slippery stones and gravel. The fastest riders used dramatic sideways slides and mid-air jumps as part of their race-winning technique.

By the late 1970s, the major bicycle makers had started to develop their own mountain bikes, marrying the fat tires common on delivery cycles of the 1920s with space-age construction technology. The first mass-produced mountain bike was the Japanese Stumpjumper, offered for sale in the United States in 1981. Since then, all the major bicycle makers have produced their own models and sales have rocketed all over the world, with the number of mountain bikers roughly doubling each year. This is causing problems of its own, especially in places where too many people are riding the same trails. The deep treads of mountain bike tires can damage grassy areas and hasten natural erosion.

◁ In the daytime, city streets are usually packed with traffic, making fast package deliveries by car or truck impossible. Many firms use bicycle messenger services as a speedy way to get their smaller packages taken across town. Many messenger riders use mountain bikes. The tough construction is as suited to potholed streets as it is to off-road trails.

Mountain bike adventures

Mountain bikes are "go-anywhere" machines. Though most people get thrills enough from cycling not too far from home, there are many adventures awaiting long-distance travelers. One of the longest trips was a 5,300 km (3,300 mile) ride to the center of Asia. In 1986, Richard and Nicholas Crane rode specially built Raleigh bikes on the 58-day trip. The route included mountains, desert and desolate country. The Cranes battled through all weathers, from torrential rain and snow blizzards to searing 46°C (115°F) sunshine. They traveled dangerously light, taking no tent, no food and only a liter (1.8 pints) water container each. To save weight, they went to extraordinary lengths. They cut the labels off their underwear, snipped the edges off their maps and drilled holes in their tools!

Other epic trips for the Cranes have included a ride of 5,790 m (19,000 ft) up the slopes of Mt. Kilimanjaro in Africa. But this was just a practice for Nick Crane's ambition for the 21st century. He wants to cycle up the 23,790 m (78,000 ft) slope of the biggest known volcano in the Solar System – Olympus Mons, on the planet Mars!

Faster and faster

Much more efficient than a standard bicycle is a type called a "recumbent." In one of these, the rider sits on a reclining seat, with legs pointing forward, feet on front-mounted pedals. Because of the low riding position, there is little air resistance and it takes less energy to keep the machine moving at speed. At 32 km/h (20 mph), a recumbent rider pedals with 20 percent less effort than someone in an upright position.

Even speedier than recumbents are human-powered vehicles, or HPVs. These have streamlined bodywork to cut air resistance to the minimum. The record for HPVs is over 105 km/h (65 mph), a speed impossible to achieve on a normal bicycle.

Unfortunately, HPVs are not really suited to crowded highways. They tend to become unsteady in sidewinds. And because they are so low, it is difficult for drivers of cars and trucks to see them in heavy traffic. Recumbents have the same problem, and some riders use high-mounted lights or flags to mark their position.

Though HPVs can make very high speeds, the fastest bike of all is in fact a specially built racing machine of standard design. On July 20, 1985, American rider John Howard reached 245.08 km/h (152 mph). He achieved this speed riding close behind a vehicle carrying a big wind shield to protect him from the air blast as he got up to speed. More help was given by "drafting," making use of the suction effect you get when following a moving vehicle closely.

▷ The reclining seat position of recumbents and HPVs has some disadvantages, not least of which is that you can't stand on the pedals when climbing steep hills. The HPV shown on the right is the *Gold Rush America*, which set a 200 m (656 ft) dash record of 105.39 km/h (65.34 mph).

△ Recumbents and HPVs may be the leading edge of bicycle design, but standard bikes make ideal transportation, especially in poor parts of the world. And successful design features are eventually included on many lesser bikes. Much of the world depends on the bicycle. In China, where the photograph above was taken, about 200 million bikes provide the main means of personal transportation. All across Asia, cycle-rickshaws (known as trishaws) are popular as taxis, for carrying firewood, furniture, farm animals and almost anything else which can fit aboard.

Future bike

*T*he bicycle is a "mature" product. Over a long period, it has been improved to the point where dramatic advances are no longer likely. However, there are exciting times ahead for the bike. Pollution concerns, traffic congestion, fitness, fashion and new construction materials are all playing a part in increasing the role of the bicycle in the 1990s.

Congested city streets could make more people see the sense in returning to two wheels as a way of beating the traffic jams. Three quarters of all urban journeys are less than 8 km (5 miles), trips on which using a bicycle is likely to be quicker than driving a car. To combine a fast journey with no parking problems and getting some healthy exercise as well must make sense, even to the most enthusiastic car driver.

New materials under development will allow high tech frames and other components to be made. Magnesium, a very light and strong metal, is beginning to be used for frames weighing just 2.2 kg (5 lb). Just as important, magnesium allows frames to be cast in one piece from molten metal. This method is much faster and cheaper than the traditional way of cutting and welding together lengths of metal tubing to form a rigid diamond frame. Other modern materials include carbon fiber and various plastics, all lighter and stronger than standard tubes.

On these pages you can see ideas for two bikes which could be developed in the 1990s. The lightweight roadster has disk wheels and a built-in lighting system for night riding. The all-terrain machine is designed for police patrol work.

△ A growing number of police forces find that mountain bikes make a good replacement for foot patrols and can be used to chase criminals long after cars have had to stop – along narrow alleys and on rough ground for example. This design for a future police bike includes puncture-proof tires, a siren, and an equipment cylinder mounted behind the seat.

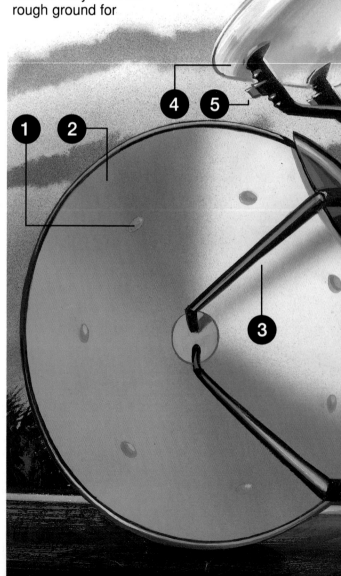

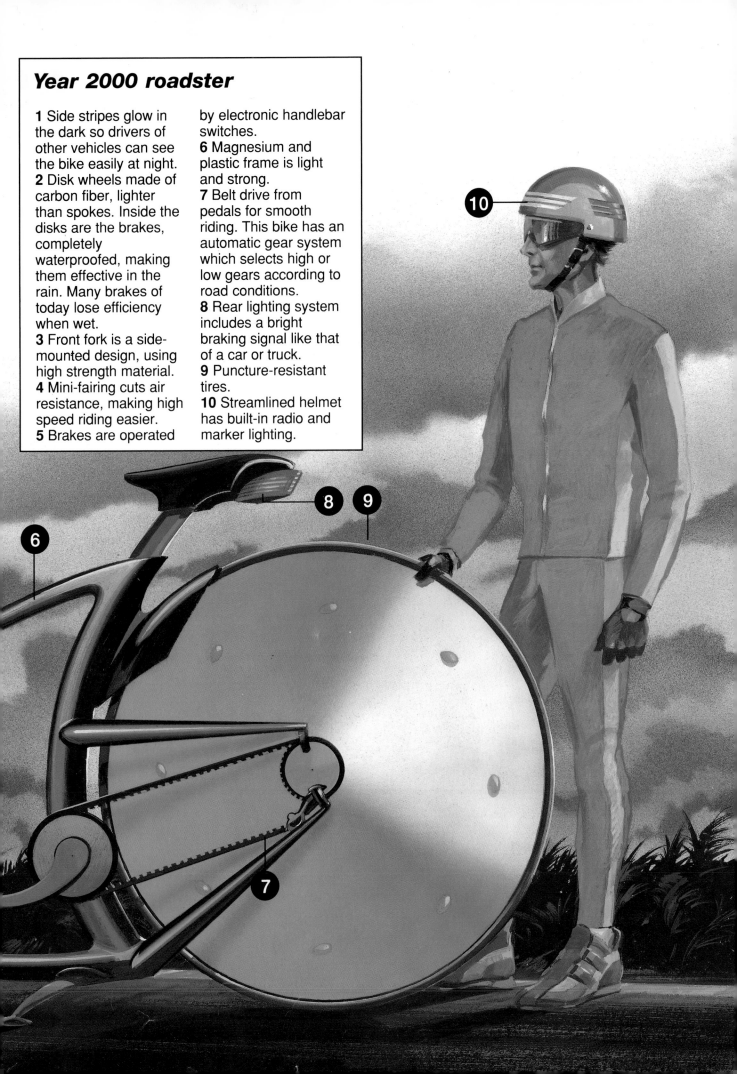

Year 2000 roadster

1 Side stripes glow in the dark so drivers of other vehicles can see the bike easily at night.
2 Disk wheels made of carbon fiber, lighter than spokes. Inside the disks are the brakes, completely waterproofed, making them effective in the rain. Many brakes of today lose efficiency when wet.
3 Front fork is a side-mounted design, using high strength material.
4 Mini-fairing cuts air resistance, making high speed riding easier.
5 Brakes are operated by electronic handlebar switches.
6 Magnesium and plastic frame is light and strong.
7 Belt drive from pedals for smooth riding. This bike has an automatic gear system which selects high or low gears according to road conditions.
8 Rear lighting system includes a bright braking signal like that of a car or truck.
9 Puncture-resistant tires.
10 Streamlined helmet has built-in radio and marker lighting.

Bicycle progress

O n these pages you can see 150 years of bicycle development, from Macmillan's two-wheeler to the fast three-wheel Windcheetah recumbent of the 1980s.

▷ Kirkpatrick Macmillan's velocipede of 1839 had a pedal, rod and crank system to turn the back wheel. It worked well, but Macmillan's ideas were largely unknown outside Scotland and his machine was not developed any further.

△ The Premier was one of a number of safety bikes made around 1885. It looked very like a modern machine, with both wheels nearly the same size and an adjustable saddle. The frame was similar to a modern diamond pattern.

▽ Described as "the most comfortable bicycle ever designed," the 1904 Dursley Pederson had a hammock saddle made of silk cord. The frame was made of very thin tubes, arranged in pairs.

△ In 1870, the Ariel bicycle was introduced by James Starley and William Hillman of Coventry. It was the first recognizable high wheel machine and had adjustable spokes to keep the wheel perfectly balanced.

◁ In 1933, the firm of Arnold, Schwinn and Co. introduced the Streamline Aerocycle, "built like an airplane fuselage." The fat-tired machine weighed in at a hefty 30 kg (70 lb). The similar Schwinn Black Phantom shown here is now a rare collector's item.

▽ The 1977 Bickerton marks a high point in folding bike design. It weighs just 8 kg (18 lb) and can be carried in a trunk or large carrying case. Various versions are still made, for city use or country cruising.

▷ The 1940 BSA folding bike was made for use by airborne troops in World War II. Folding the bike was easy - you just loosened two wing nuts and slung the machine over your shoulder.

△ The Raleigh Chopper was popular in the 1970s. It had a center-mounted gear shift and a shock-absorbing spring under the long "banana" seat.

▽ The Windcheetah SL is one of the best recumbents. Nicknamed the "Speedy," it has won contests in the United States, Canada and Europe. Cruising at 32 km/h (20 mph) is easy on flat surfaces, with 64 km/h (40 mph) possible on gentle downhills.

Facts and records

Since the invention of the bicycle, a fascinating variety of riders and machines has taken to the roads. Here are some interesting facts about them and the way in which the world of cycling has developed over the years.

The first known design for a bicycle is thought to have been created by Italian inventor and artist Leonardo da Vinci. In about 1490, he produced a small sketch like the one above, with many of the features of a modern machine. Some experts think one of Leonardo's pupils may have produced the drawing.

The first race champion was British rider James Moore. On May 31, 1868, he won a 2 km (1.24 mile) velocipede race, held in St. Cloud Park in Paris. This was the first bicycle race ever held.

In 1881, there were only five bicycles in Moscow, yet police were so worried about cyclists' bad riding that they banned riding in the city.

On April 22, 1884, American Thomas Stevens left San Francisco on a high wheel bicycle to ride around the world. At one point across the United States he was cornered by a mountain lion. In Paris he cycled down the Champs Elysees. From France, he cycled east, through Europe and across Turkey. A year after leaving San Francisco he languished in jail, having been arrested in Afghanistan, but was soon freed and by August 1886, had reached India, shown on the right. October saw him cruising along the dirt tracks of Canton in China. A ferry boat took him to Japan and when he had completed his high riding there, he caught a ship across the Pacific Ocean, back home to the United States. He arrived on January 4, 1887, nearly three years after leaving. His epic trip inspired many others, including John Foster Frazer who completed a 30,779 km (19,083 mile) world trip in the mid-1890s in 774 days. The current record for a round-the-world trip is held by British rider Nicholas Sanders, who managed it in just over 78 days. Distances and routes vary for these long distance journeys though, so times are not strictly comparable.

The first air-filled pneumatic tires were fitted by John Boyd Dunlop to his son's Quadrant machine on February 28, 1888.

The longest bicycle of the 19th century was the 1896 *Decemptuple* tandem. This American machine could seat ten riders, one behind the other. It was beaten in 1979, by a group of Belgian cycle enthusiasts. Their 35-seater measured 20.4 m (67 ft) in length and weighed 1,100 kg (2,425 lb). The smallest bicycle is one made by Australian Neville Patten in 1988. His tiny bike has wheels just 1.95 cm (0.76 in) in diameter.

In 1913, the front forks of Eugene Christophe's bike snapped in two. He was leader in the Tour de France at the time, and rather than giving up the race, he put the bike on his shoulders and ran 11 km (7 miles) to the nearest village. There he found a blacksmith's forge and repaired the bike. He finished the race, but was given penalty points because a small boy pumped the blacksmith's bellows. The rules of the race allowed no help at all. Today, the rules are different, and Tour riders are followed by

vehicles carrying mechanics and spares. Riders who break down expect to be back on the road in moments.

On September 30, 1928, Belgian cyclist Leon Vanderstuyft covered a distance of 122.78 km (76.1 miles) in one hour. This record still stands as the best one-hour distance from a standing start.

Among the odder cycling records is that achieved by Belgian Rudi De Greef in 1982. On November 19, he cycled absolutely nowhere, managing to remain completely stationary, without putting a foot on the ground, for ten hours.

▷ This 19th century advertising poster for the Diamant bicycle firm of Germany shows two ladies wearing bloomers, a clothing style more suited to bicycle riding than the formal dresses of the time. The bicycles are equipped with front brakes, mudguards and comfortable sprung saddles.

John Howard's top speed record of 1985 was achieved with help from a windshield and the drafting effect of following a vehicle closely. Other riders have also made use of this effect, including a group of British time-trial riders. In 1976,

△ The *Decemptuple* tandem of 1896 shows off its paces.

they broke ten records while riding on a busy highway. Big container trucks hurtling by, sucked the riders along in their wake, giving a speed boost.

Bicycle technology

This glossary explains many of the technical terms used in this book.

ATB
All-terrain bicycle, more often called a mountain bike.

BMX
Bicycle motocross, a form of off-road racing using small wheeled machines with thick tires and strong frames.

Caliper brakes
These work by pinching the metal rim of a wheel between two rubber brake blocks. Can be either center pull or side pull types. Mountain bikes use cantilever brakes which give more room either side of the wheel, so mud is not easily trapped around the brake pads.

Carbon fiber
Material which has small fibers or "hairs" of carbon added for strength. Base material into which the carbon is mixed is typically some form of plastic. Carbon fiber is light but strong.

▽ Derailleur gears are the most popular on sports, touring and mountain bikes. This diagram shows how they work.

Chain
Used to connect pedals to rear wheel. Various forms of chain have been tried over the years. Roller chains are used today, which use bushes or floating rollers in each link to reduce friction between the parts.

Derailleur gear
Commonly used on sports and mountain bikes. Has two sets of gear cogs, one at the pedals, one at the rear wheel. Levers control which set of gears the chain links to. Low gears are used for starting and hill climbing, higher gears for cruising and high speeds.

Fairing
A rounded bodyshell which allows moving air to flow smoothly around a cyclist, so giving a streamlined effect when used on a bicycle such as a recumbent or HPV.

Front forks
Sloping twin tubes which join handlebars to front wheel.

Frame
The diamond shaped "skeleton" of a bike, to which handlebars, pedals, saddle and wheels are attached. Usually made of metal tubing, welded together to make it tough and almost unbreakable in normal use.

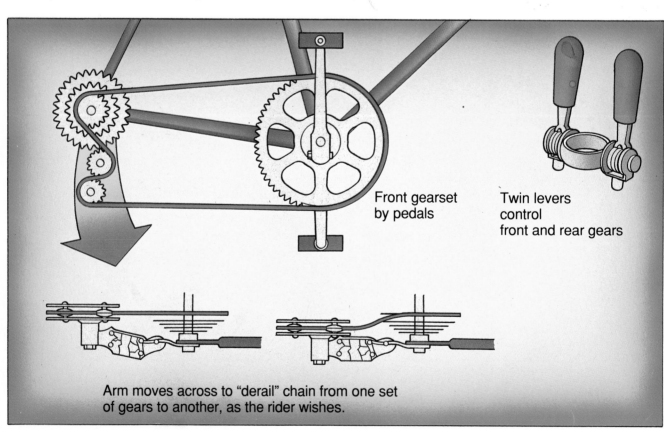

Front gearset
by pedals

Twin levers
control
front and rear gears

Arm moves across to "derail" chain from one set
of gears to another, as the rider wishes.

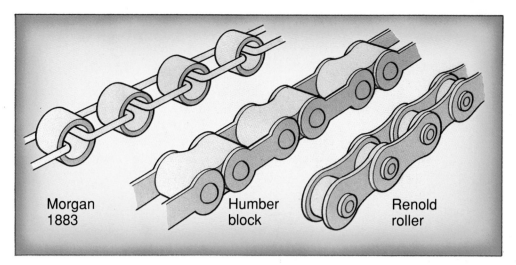

Morgan
1883

Humber
block

Renold
roller

ride by means of the "bounce" as the tire gets briefly squashed when passing over bumps. Spokes also help the ride, as they absorb shocks. Racing tires are thin-section, with air pumped in at high pressure. Shopping and mountain bike tires are thick and squashy. Touring bikes have tires midway between.

△ Like the other parts of a bicycle, chains have been developed and improved over the years.

Freewheel
A mechanism that allows the pedals to stay still or be turned backward while a bike goes downhill or coasts to a halt. Some bikes have a hub-mounted coaster brake instead of a freewheel. Here, pressing backward on the pedals operates the back brake. A problem with this is that it is very easy to skid the back wheel.

Gear
The arrangement of cogs of different sizes which enables the back wheel of a bicycle to turn at a different speed to the pedals.

▷ Most bike brakes work on the same principle, that of squeezing the wheel rim between a pair of rubber composition brake blocks. Here are two types of caliper brake, with side and center pull action.

HPV
Human powered vehicle, usually a streamlined recumbent, with either two or three wheels.

Hub gear
Usually with just three speeds, a hub gear is contained in a small cylinder at the rear wheel hub. Such gears are very reliable and need little attention, just

an occasional drop of oil and minor adjustment from time to time. Mostly used on basic "city bikes."

Ordinary
High wheel bicycle of the 19th century, also known as a penny-farthing.

Pneumatic tire
Any air-filled tire. Provides a cushioned

Recumbent
Type of cycle in which the rider sits back on a hammock or seat. Can have two or three wheels.

Safety
Describes the first bicycles with smaller front wheels than those of the high wheel ordinary machines. The Rover of 1884 was the first safety bike.

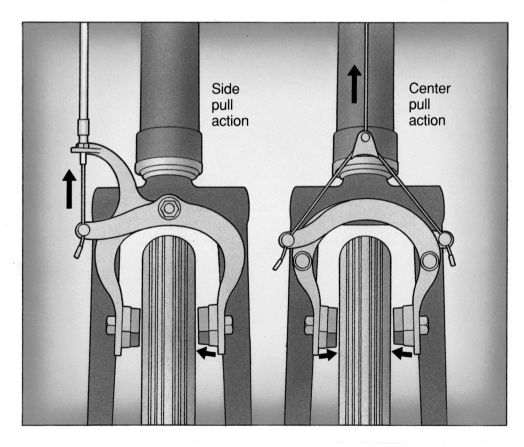

Side pull action

Center pull action

Index

PRINTED IN BELGIUM BY

proost
INTERNATIONAL BOOK PRODUCTION